VINTAGE LIVING

etro style for today's homes

TAVERNE AGENCY

TERRA

THE AUTHORS

As the founder of Taverne Agency, **Nathalie Taverne** has spent the past eleven years working with the world's finest interior, lifestyle and food photographers, ensuring their work appears in the world's finest magazines. Within the Taverne collection, original and inspirational homes from around the world are brought together under one roof, with the stories of those who design and live in them as fascinating as the photographs are beautiful. Nathalie and her husband and business partner Robert Borghuis live and work in Amsterdam and together find time to raise their two children, Elena and John.

Having begun her writing career on the *Financial Times*' award-winning *How To Spend It* magazine, **Anna Lambert** went on to spend three years working in the Netherlands, where she began her collaboration with Nathalie Taverne. Anna's work has appeared in interiors magazines worldwide, including *Australian Vogue Living*, *World of Interiors*, *Elle Decoration* and *Elle Wonen*, and she is the author of *Easy Living* and *Inspirational Apartments*, both published by Terra Lannoo. She lives with her husband and two daughters in the UK.

© 2010 Uitgeverij Terra Lannoo B.V.
P.O.Box 614, 6800 AP Arnhem
The Netherlands
info@terralannoo.nl
www.terralannoo.nl
Uitgeverij Terra is part of the Lannoo group, Belgium

TEXT AND IMAGES: © 2010 Taverne Agency B.V.
Lisdoddelaan 79
1087 KB Amsterdam
The Netherlands
www.taverneagency.com

COMPILATION: Nathalie Taverne
TEXT: Anna Lambert
DESIGN: Manon Jansen for Pier 3 Creatie, Lelystad
PRINTED AND BOUND: Leo Paper Products Ltd., Hong Kong

ISBN 978 90 8989 206 5
NUR 454
Also published in Dutch as Vintage
(ISBN 978 90 8989 192 1)

THE ENDURING APPEAL

Just what is it about the vintage look that lures so many of us, encouraging us to give it expression within our own homes? Firstly, it's that so many different styles fall within that one category – you can go back as far as two hundred years if you want to recreate a shabby-chic look that all's about battered antique furniture, faded damask, embroidered textiles and delicate chandeliers. Alternatively, look to the 1950s if you love pastel colours, mirrors and steel, or turn to the 1970s for inspiration if your tastes veer more towards the glam-rock era. In an increasingly homogenous world, choosing vintage allows us to inject one-off style into our homes, to personalise them with pre-loved pieces that aren't going to be available to the masses – even if they were in the past. By evoking a sense of history, the vintage interior succeeds in making us feel more comfortable and secure – more 'at home'. Building displays of vintage possessions, meanwhile, allows us to indulge our desire both to create and to collect.

The vintage look, too, is one that can be successfully achieved whatever the home-owners' budget – yes, there are valuable classics to be acquired: original Panton light fittings, Eames chairs, Corbusier chaise longues – but there are excellent reproductions on offer, too, as well as pieces that, though they may owe their inspiration to the design masters, are far more affordable than originals. Meanwhile, charity shops, thrift stores, flea markets, boot fairs and internet auction sites such as ebay all offer chances to pick up beautiful, cheerful or just plain quirky pieces at bargain prices. The uniqueness of what's available means the vintage home can't be put together quickly, and that's something that only adds to its charm. It's a place that, clearly, has evolved – it's been built up slowly with love, care and patience. As such, it will always seem a world away from the show-home 'buy-it-all-in-a-weekend' approach that modern design stores and flat-pack furniture manufacturers would often appear to endorse. The biggest challenge is to put vintage pieces together in a way that delights, rather than confuses, the eye. Within the pages that follow you'll find examples of every sort of vintage home, in which serenity, playfulness and order have all been achieved. You can be sure you won't see any other homes like them, so take inspiration. For, if we're to create homes that truly reflect our own personalities, we can all learn from the message of the vintage home: it's both possible and pleasurable to create ultra-personal interiors that are as unique as those who live in them.

OF VINTAGE

From Baroque glamour to rough-and-ready simplicity, these area
in the home can encompass every variation on the vintage theme

LIVING
SPACES

THE COURAGE OF YOUR CONVICTIONS

The secret to making vintage work in the modern interior is simple: choose only what works for you, what you love to live with and what'll make you feel truly 'at home'.

If theatricality is your style, it's a good idea to keep at least one element of the room uncomplicated, or the overall effect may be overwhelming. In this London living room, for instance, the plain white walls, wooden floor and painted brick fireplace not only reflect light, ensuring the room appears more spacious, they also serve as a simple foil to the classic 70s' disco ball hanging from the ceiling and to the battered chesterfield that dominates the room. A capacious, comfortable sofa should be the key piece in any living room. 'Take care when choosing vintage pieces that they can in fact be resprung and refurbished if necessary – who wants to be stuck with a sofa that looks great but is uncomfortable to sit on?'

Simple backgrounds and colour palettes allow more flamboyant pieces in living rooms to come into their own – whether it's the elaborate table shown left, or the original 70s' peacock rattan chairs on the following page. Use texture to add interest – in this home, vintage crocheted curtains, leather pouffes, fine bespoke fabrics and feature wallpaper all bring off-beat visual warmth to the various living areas.

COLOUR AND CURVES FOR A FEMININE FEEL

Rococo details, rich colours and lavish trimmings will give any room an opulent vibe.

For a new lease of life, vintage pieces often benefit from a bit of customising: fringing can be added to soft furnishings such as cushions, curtains and sofas, while furniture can be updated or rethought with a lick of paint. In the image right, the look is all about working with one rich palette of reds, from deep burgundy to softer pink. Variation is introduced through pattern and texture, which is where the smaller details can make all the difference. When building up your own vintage pieces, go for finishes that contrast with one another: think of exposed brickwork next to heavy velvet, damask silk on top of wood. A vintage chair can be given an entirely fresh look by reupholstering it in an unexpected fabric – think 50s' florals or

contemporary graphic prints. The difference is in the details, so whether you choose to paint a wooden floor in dramatic black or red, or to combine a collection of thrift-shop paintings in a certain way, it's all about your choices and your style. A sense of integrity that sees you stay true to your own tastes will ensure your home will always say more about you than it does about any one particular fashion.

If your tastes are decidedly feminine, look for vintage crystal lamp-bases, delicate, curlicued wrought iron and elaborate furniture.

Such pieces can often be found very inexpensively at charity shops and flea markets.

INDUSTRIAL MEETS VINTAGE

Transforming industrial spaces into appealing homes presents particular challenges. The secret of success is to work with the building you've got – don't try to pretend it's anything other than what it is.

In the New York loft shown opposite, the owner has emphasised the utilitarian feel of the space by choosing an equally workaday wall decoration: a vast, extraordinary old metal door, whose many-hued, rough-and-ready patina echoes the rough-and-ready feel of the space. Salvage yards and reclamation centres are just the sort of places to find such pieces. Do check in advance, though, that your wall and floor can cope with anything particularly heavy – and that you've got the necessary man-power to install it. The two photos that follow show that it's worth celebrating the industrial heritage of a home – here, pipes and beams are painted and left as an integral part of the building, not hidden away. Just as a luxurious leather belt can lift a simple

cotton dress, quality vintage pieces will always elevate the look of any home. In this loft, for instance, the owner has mixed thrift-store finds with classic investments such as Charles and Ray Eames' iconic RAR rocker of 1950, Marcel Wanders' Bottoni sofa and a fantastical rug by Scottish company Timorous Beasties. A frequent hallmark of the vintage home-maker is a willingness to mix a variety of things from different periods together – in this home, for instance, the spanking modern Wanders' sofa sits next to a traditional green leather chesterfield – and to improvise where necessary. Overleaf, the owner of this loft space found himself with left-over snippets of designer wallpaper, so pieced them together to create a patchwork effect.

COLOURFUL RETRO WEDS CONTEMPORARY DESIGN

In this fabulous Palm Springs apartment, the owners have cleverly combined vintage classics with the latest designs, also adding their own creations into the mix, for a style that they term 'happy chic'.

The biggest challenge in creating a vintage interior is to get the balance right: to have sufficient pieces in your home to create a coherent theme rather than a look that shouts 'I've just come back from the flea market.' That's where choosing one piece to begin with can be useful – you could, for instance, use a picture or a wonderful vintage fabric as a basis for a colour scheme, or build up a collection of pottery based on finds from a particular ceramicist you admire. In this home, the balance couldn't be better: in the dining area a marble-topped Sarinen table – a classic of its kind – has been teamed with 60s' French chairs. Bringing the look bang up to date, though, is their reupholstery: Alexander Girard's Double

Triangles fabric for Maharam has a retro vibe but 21st-century properties too. Above the table, another vintage find in the form of the 1960s' lamp is testament to the variety of period chandeliers available – this one falls decidedly into the 'groovy', as opposed to shabby chic, category. In a limited space, what's particularly clever is the way in which a transparent screen has been used to separate eating and sitting areas – it's a trick you could apply in your own home if you're short of space. Many screens come with castors so you can move them around as required – and here, two back-to-back Philippe Starck Ghost mirrors add a burst of chartreuse to the colour scheme and allow space-enhancing light to reflect around the room.

Light, pattern, scale and colour all find expression within both vintage and 21st-century furnishings

for a look that's as lively and energising as it is easy to live with.

In the seating area (previous page), it's clear how a rug can anchor various pieces within a room – here bringing together Jonathan Adler's Boxer sofas and lacquered tables with a pair of vintage white armchairs by Marco Zaanuso. Picking up on the colours and shapes of the Ojai wall tiles (also by ceramicist Jonathan Adler, whose home this is) are textiles over the chairs by the Swedish artist Petra Bomer.

If you're building a collection of ceramics, take a tip from the living areas shown here and stick perhaps to just one shade. You can enliven it by introducing a vibrant colour with a retro vibe such as orange, plum or olive green. Though some of the pieces here were designed by Jonathan Adler, playful vintage treasures picked up locally and inexpensively include lamps and the large china dog who waits patiently by the door. Play with number and scale within your collection too – oversized pieces can add an unexpected touch to a display, while items grouped in threes will always look more comfortable than items arranged regimentally in symmetrical twos.

SERENE IN CREAMS AND PASTELS

Often unashamedly romantic, pale colours can make a great choice for living spaces, where they'll convey a restful sense of calm.

One of the easiest ways to build up an uncomplicated vintage look is to pick all your colours from the paler end of the spectrum. While pure white on its own can look striking, it's a tricky one to get right – depending on the light in the room, it can also appear cold or dirty. Cream is an easier option – a colour that will always bring subtle richness and depth. It's easy to add variation to your given shade simply by choosing furniture and accessories in a variety of textures and finishes. If shabby-chic is your style, use damask or embroidered cushions, throws and curtains, white-washed wood and capacious Gustavian-style furniture, adding aubusson rugs, plenty of foxed mirror and pretty chandeliers to complete the look. For a more contemporary alternative, team cream with classic 20th-century furniture from the likes of Eames, Panton and Corbusier if your budget will stretch that far – or simply take inspiration from the clean lines of their designs and see what you can find in local furnishing stores and auctions. Keep other key elements simple: opt for Roman blinds or shutters, natural-wood flooring and unfussy accessories – Scandinavian glass from the 1950s and 60s, for instance, with its pure colours and graphic shapes, makes a great choice.

A creamy colour scheme is here teamed with mis-matched furniture, floral prints and chandeliers

creating a look that's both relaxed and full of low-key period charm.

ADD A DASH OF JUICY COLOUR

Introduce bright, bold shades to a backdrop of white and you've got the recipe for a fresh, fun and modern vintage look.

Whether you're creating a vintage look in your own home or rented accommodation, adding interest via colourful accessories is easy and inexpensive. Another plus is that, whatever you choose to decorate – a piece of furniture, say, or an artwork – will be portable and usually small enough to repaint if and when you fancy a change. Again, the key to making a success of this look is to keep the setting simple – but you can inject colour into any home, regardless of its architectural period or size. As far as accessories are concerned, man-made materials take colour particularly well. On the right, for instance, the owner has decided to make a feature of these two original Panton Flowerpot lights – and

who can blame her, especially given that their colours echo the rounded shapes and citrus shades of her own-design ceramics. When it comes to furniture, it is possible to mix pieces from different periods – providing every piece chosen has a simple silhouette, there's no reason why an old French walnut cupboard, say, shouldn't work with some 1950s' plywood chairs. Children's artwork is something else that can work brilliantly in this sort of vintage home – its naive style and vibrancy will always create an impact, regardless of whether small pieces are displayed individually or combined for a feature-wall-cum-gallery effect. Alternatively, you can create feature walls by opting for one strong paint colour or by using any

Whether you eat in it, chat in it, work in it or chill in it there's a vintage style for every kind of room.

The fun, off-beat vintage look can work really well in family homes. Here, classic pieces from the 1950s and 60s combine brilliantly with kids' artwork and brightly painted wooden furniture.

of the multitude of intricate and graphic wallpapers – plenty of which are works of art in their own right – now available. Another simple idea is to paint furniture using high gloss in a primary colour – the chest of drawers on the left, for instance, has been painted to complement both the Eames chair and the work on the wall so that the three pieces form a little vignette within the room. Such techniques also succeed in isolating given areas – something that's important within living spaces in which many different activities may take place. So if your living room also functions as a study, for instance, you can 'mark off' a corner of the room by picking pieces for it that are all of the same colour – specifically, one that's

different from other elements of the room. Although a wooden floor will always bring an uncluttered, timeless feel to a room, it's worth considering carpet – both for comfort underfoot and, depending on what design you opt for, its retro appeal. With so many colours and designs available, the options are limitless. Just be sure to choose something you'll be happy to live with for a long time...

WHERE THE LIVING IS GROOVY

Team lacquered surfaces, graphic prints and statement colours with pieces taken from the 1960s and 1970s and you've got a look that manages to be both retro and of the moment at one and the same time.

The great thing about the vintage home is that it can take on so many guises – and the look of this 1960s-built South American villa is a world away from 'shabby chic' style. Instead the owners have plumped for a few key pieces, such as the Arne Jacobsen Swan chair, and have added their own-design textiles, vintage cushions and bespoke square-lined sofas (by design company and store Micasa of São Paulo), which themselves have a 1970s' feel. Echoing the gloss of that era is the floor that runs throughout the main reception room and TV den: it's made from light-reflecting white polished polyurethane resin. Furniture, too, is lacquered: a fibre-glass coffee table and a Jasper Morrison bench.

The purpose of each room will of course dictate the furnishings within different living spaces. In this home, while the reception room has a cool, laid-back feel, the informal TV room has a decidedly playful vibe. Trinkets collected from travels around the world, and particularly Japan, reflect the owners' love of kitsch, while a wall-mounted surfboard is testament to one of their favourite hobbies. With a den that's been designed primarily for comfort, the inclusion of an easy-to-reach vintage fridge – handy for a beer while watching TV – makes perfect sense.

THE WARMTH OF WOOD

If you're the sort of person who finds it easier to decorate by sticking to one material, you can do a lot worse than choosing wood. It comes in a variety of hues and patinas and will bring warmth, in every sense of the word, to any vintage living space. What's not to like?

In this Australian home, simple marine plywood has been used to introduce a sense of warmth to an otherwise industrial-feeling space. Furniture here not only includes classic pieces such as the Eames rocker and Isamu Nouguchi's 1947-designed coffee table (pictured overleaf) but also a 1950s' daybed. Every country has its own company renowned for producing these sorts of simple, utilitarian domestic pieces – Ercol in the UK for instance – and such names have become highly collectable. Non-branded furniture from the same era, though, and featuring the same simple lines can be picked up inexpensively and easily from charity furniture warehouses and small general auctions. Wooden floors can lend a cosy, rustic look to vintage rooms – but a vast expanse of wood can make furniture seem 'lost'. That's when it's wise to introduce rugs into the mix, not only to 'anchor' various items of furniture within a room but also to add interest and texture – as well, of course, as providing warmth underfoot. Where space is at a premium, there's no excuse not to go to town with displays of any collections you've built up: choose from wall-mounting them via shelves or showing them off on the tops of sideboards or on individual plinths.

Vintage style brings intimacy
EVEN IN LARGE SPACES

Here, warm wood finishes and statement pictures combine with a wealth of small-scale displays. These draw the eye into the room, creating a homey feel even within this vast industrial building.

A SENSE OF TRANQUILLITY

Empty walls create a feeling of openness,
while Chinese statuettes and an all-seeing Buddha
add to a soothing atmosphere.

If in doubt, keep it simple and you can't go wrong. In this room, for example, everything has a purpose: to please the eye or to provide comfort. There's not much here, but what there is has been very carefully selected – the prototype 1960s' Parisian daybed, the Californian footstool. The owner is well aware, though, that this approach to vintage style can look overly austere – and that's one of the reasons why she's painted the wall facing the one shown here in a sensuous shade of olive green. Elsewhere in the apartment, a dining area sees a contemporary table teamed with vintage chairs and a feature wall enlivened by the intricate pattern of Cole & Son's Cow Parsley wallpaper. In the work room, meanwhile, a splash of orange comes courtesy of a sideboard that originally graced an office in New York's Chrysler Building. On top of it sit objects that appeal to the owner – a vintage radio and Fornasetti fish plate were discovered at the flea market in New York, which just goes to prove that there are still vintage bargains to be had out there if you're prepared to persevere until you find them.

Sven Sandström

Le monde imagi
d'Odilon Redon

Edmund Engelman

UND FREUD

ASSE 19, VIENNA

UNIVERSE

arlbo gh New Y rk

A mood board doesn't necessarily have to consist of pictures that inspire you.

On the left is the owner's collection of art books, which she regularly turns to for visual inspiration.

LIVING SPONTANEOUSLY

A vintage home can be completely uncontrived – for some people it's all about what comes together and when, and how they can create a world for themselves that's easy to be a part of.

If bright-and-breezy is your style, you'll love a vintage look that's all about slowly, haphazardly accumulating pieces over the years – after all, isn't that just how it goes in the happiest family homes? In this den, it's clear that the owners have taken into account what the room's primarily used for: storage of surfing gear. To this end, they've created wall-mounted fixtures for surfboards and plenty of hanging space. They've also stuck to matting as a hard-wearing, inexpensive flooring material. Beyond that, though, there are no rules: it's clear it's home to pieces they've selected simply because they love them, whether it's a classic standard lamp or an old bamboo cabinet. And that's what's so refreshing about this space – though it might appear to house an indiscriminate collection of possessions, what links them is that they all mean something to the owners.

In the same home, the sitting room (pictured overleaf) is a great example of how different zones can be created using a variety of vintage pieces within one room. Here, you'll find a table for eating or working at, cosy corners for reading, seating close to both the fireplace and the TV, plus seating that offers the best possible views through the large picture window. Art ties in the various colours of the room and traditional fabrics are used in unexpected ways – the sofa is covered with thick cord while the wing chairs have been reupholstered using old army blankets. Furniture here includes everything from antiques to 1950s' chairs but, again, what succesfully unites the look is the owners' relaxed approach – from the way the pieces have been put together, it's clear that this is a room designed primarily for comfort and relaxation. It's a room to truly feel 'at home' in.

Give as much consideration to the practical as you do to the aesthetic and it's certainly possible to create a vintage-style kitchen that's fit for the 21st century.

KITCHENS

SOFTENING ANY HARD EDGES

In this kitchen, the owner has gone for the 'less is more' approach with very few pieces in the room. Here it's all about quality, not quantity – and the result is a working space that still maintains a retro feel.

If you start with a space that consists of a simple shell – as in this kitchen, with its plain white walls and a high-gloss dark-chocolate wooden floor – adding a few vintage touches is a great way to raise the room from a mere place for working to somewhere with character. After all, kitchens, like bathrooms, are mainly practical spaces with a clearly-defined function and, as such, it's all too easy for their design to look, and feel, overly clinical and cold. What's clever about this particular kitchen is the way in which the owners have stuck to 21st-century mod-cons (the cooker and fridge, for example) but added flashes of vintage – the vivid orange kettle, the chairs at the table, the old rug on the floor and

the 60s'-style clock. It's a great way of bringing a pared-down retro style to the room without going 'the whole hog'. Yes, it's possible for die-hard vintage fans to purchase reconditioned cookers and fridges from specialist suppliers (check ebay or your local salvage yard for details of what may be available), but they're expensive, are likely to be inefficient in comparison to 21st-century models and, if they break down, it can be difficult to find replacement parts for them. Besides, with so many retro-styled contemporary models on the market – those curvaceous and capacious Smeg fridges, for instance – it's possible to purchase the best of both worlds. In some cases, particularly where work surfaces are concerned, vintage

Sometimes less is more – here, just a few useful pots made from roughly-hewn wood sit on a wooden shelf.

They provide a striking, rustic contrast to the minimalist 1960s'-style wall clock next to them.

furnishings have much to offer – an old butcher's block, piece of wood or marble will have the character of age, but will still be highly serviceable. Elsewhere, when it comes to storage space, it's still possible to find 1950s' formica pantry-cupboards – often in pastel shades such as lemon or baby blue – that open up to reveal drawers, cupboards, cup hooks and a work surface. If you don't want to furnish your own kitchen with such pieces, there are plenty of unfitted kitchen options available – and such pieces will always have more of a vintage feel than the sleek, high-gloss, fitted kitchens of today. If the rustic vintage look is more your style, stick to natural materials with integrity: wood, stone, slate and brick all look at home

and, because of their timelessness, it's hard to pin them down to any specific era. Add a few retro accessories such as a set of pretty tins, an old spice cabinet or perhaps an assortment of mismatched china. Then introduce traditional fabrics – perhaps by lining glass cupboard doors with pleated gingham – and you've created a vintage country look easily and inexpensively.

WHERE EACH PIECE STANDS ALONE

In the eating area of this kitchen, it's about the impression every item creates individually rather than the visual whole – and the result is a pleasing eclecticism.

Undoubtedly we're seeing a visual hotchpotch here, but it works because the predominant colour in the room comes via the white of the floor and walls. To prevent this look from appearing too cold, it's essential to bring some playful elements into the mix, and the room is enlivened by the green of the plant and the rich tones of the portrait of the Ghanaian football player that hangs on the wall. Other quirky elements include the Superordinate Antler lamp by local designer Jason Miller and, around the glass trestle table, the mish-mash of chairs including Philippe Starck's Ghost chair, a chair complete with castors by Nikolai Moderbacher and a Redstr/collective chair with its distinctive rubber-stamped seat.

A sense of kitsch is introduced via the plates on the wall, but in the kitchen itself the look is more practical. When not being used as a home for the collection of Jaime Hayton's white ceramic vessels, the stainless steel table can be used as a tough, no-nonsense work surface. The lamp overhead provides task lighting and was a second-hand-store find - don't forget that vintage lighting can often be revamped, rewired or modified by a qualified electrician to meet current standards.

EVERYTHING'S COMIN' UP ROSES

For the ultimate in 'girliness', a kitchen needs little more than pink paint, silver accessories, vintage portraits and a liberal dose of kitsch.

The dining area of the room was the starting point for this industrial New York apartment's transformation into Girl Heaven. The old black-painted table and yellow-cotton-upholstered chairs – probably from the early 1960s – were vintage-store finds, while the rug underneath them, by New York-based textile designer Madeline Weinrib, succeeds in both echoing the colour of the table and diluting its heaviness.

Within the kitchen itself, it's the unexpected that really catches the eye: the silk roses, glamorous oil portraits, religious paintings and statues, mirrors and animal-print curtains – the sort of things you'd expect to find in a boudoir. Plenty of zinc and stainless steel – in the form of the sink and a little cooker respectively – bring a welcome functional feel, though, preventing the area from looking completely over the top. The pretty metal cupboard – from a local antique shop – is a great example of using vintage storage in an innovative way. It's not the sort of piece one would expect to find in a kitchen and, visually, it works all the better for its unexpectedness. The owner doesn't like having to look at the detritus of cooking, so she's added lace curtains to hide the contents of the cupboard. Almost any type of cupboard can be customised to suit a kitchen or eating space – French armoires look terrific in shabby-chic vintage spaces, while old meat safes and zinc lockers are at home in industrial-style kitchens.

GETTING THE MIX RIGHT

This kitchen space works so well because of the owner's sure eye for colour – she has deftly tempered shiny surfaces of glass and stainless steel with distressed-finished painted wooden pieces and a funky mix of treasures.

In this South African home, rustic elements – the tongue-and-groove ceiling and peeling paint of the benches and table – have been infused with a touch of old-style opulence, courtesy of the chandelier. All this has been topped off with contemporary elements: glass splash-backs, a free-standing stainless-steel fridge and sleek fitted cupboards. This clever mix of finishes gives the room a warm, relaxed vibe that's complemented by the colour palette. Pistachio green mixes with the warmer tones of the floor and table to ensure a look that's cool in summer but inviting in winter. Collections on display include colourful ceramics, oversize bottles, plastic dolls and funky artwork. Use has even been made of the

door panels – here they're used to frame images of a cheeky winking character. So what is it exactly that gives this room a vintage feel? For a start, the generous proportions of the kitchen immediately say 'period architecture'. Meanwhile, the aged wood surfaces – partially stripped to reveal a variety of patinas – bring their own sense of history. Finally, the lighting is vintage at its best – an unusual mix of the classic chandelier and the ceramic globes, hanging like two art-deco earrings, which perfectly echo the colour on the walls.

THE DIFFERENCE IS IN THE DETAIL

No one could accuse the owner of this all-white kitchen of lack of commitment. All the elements have been brought together with the utmost care – from open shelving, basket work and gathered curtains to crystal and china.

The question that this sort of kitchen immediately raises for the onlooker is whether or not anyone who actually cooks in it will be able to maintain this sort of pristine finish. It'll need to be cleaned regularly, that's for sure, but, if the cupboard drapes are machine-washable and the work surfaces and floor can easily be mopped, that shouldn't prove too much of a problem. A room that looks like this will always have a restful feel. Overleaf, we can see what difference the odd vintage detail here and there can make to the kitchen-diner. The floral wallpaper used on just one feature wall brings romance to the eating area, with a birdcage and a pink-hued Victorian chandelier matching its intricacy. In the kitchen, meanwhile, it's taken just the simplest of touches to bring a vintage vibe: pink-crystal door handles (an easy finishing touch that can transform lack-lustre furniture) and a couple of wrought-iron bar stools from the 1950s. Reflective marble-and-glass work surfaces and splash-backs allow light to bounce round the room, making this a practical, pretty space in which to work and eat.

The ultimate sanctuaries within the home, these spaces
benefit from the soothing charm that vintage style can bring.

BED
& BATH
ROOMS

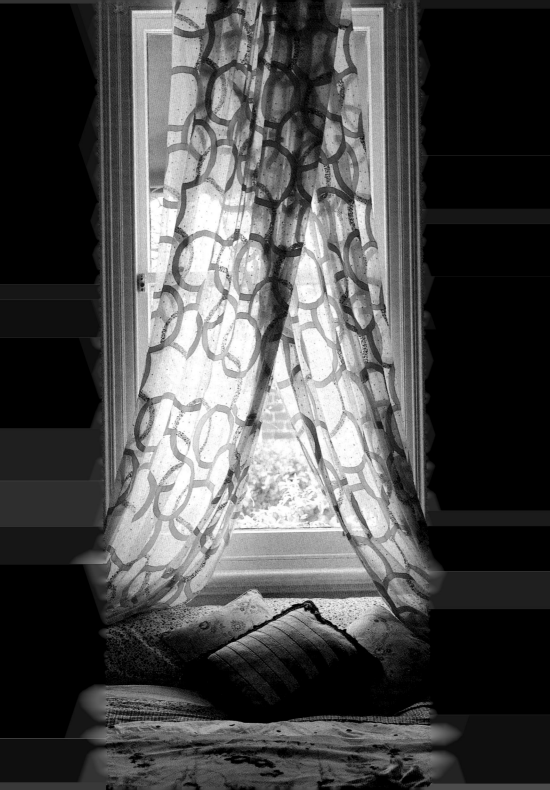

A BIT OF GIVE AND TAKE

Masculine and feminine design tastes can differ wildly when it comes to the bedroom. If your style is out of sync with that of your partner, be prepared to compromise when it comes to the vintage design of this most intimate of shared spaces.

Before embarking on designing a vintage bedroom, do consider who'll be sleeping there. If you and your partner both have feminine tastes, or if your partner is oblivious to his or her surroundings, obviously you'll have a free rein to create a room that appeals to you and you alone. On the other hand, be aware that an overly-feminine look complete with all the trimmings is unlikely to appeal to the average male. For instance, if you ask most men how they feel about cushions – as opposed to pillows – on a bed, they're likely to reply in bewildered tones 'What's the point of them?'! Hold back, then, if you love vintage boudoir style and your partner is not so keen – choose lace, glass, silks and velvets, but not all together!

Don't forget, too, that there are practical essentials that need to be included in any comfortable bedroom, whether you're creating it for yourself or your guests: a table or cabinet by the bed for books or a glass of water, a working bedside lamp and clock, additional blankets that can be removed or added according to room temperature and the best-quality pillows you can afford. Vintage down-filled eiderdowns make great accessories – they can be washed on a cool cycle and tumble-drying them is very effective in fluffing up their feathers.

VINTAGE DECADENCE

The ultimate luxury is a room with a view, where all you have to do is arise from your 1920s' French bed, open the shutters and then ease yourself into a bubble-filled, free-standing Victorian roll-top bath – bliss!

How could you fail to relax and unwind in this vast, light-filled room? Complete with its own open fireplace, this space elegantly combines bathroom with bedroom. Even if you don't have the same sort of space in your own home, by sticking to white-painted wood, simple shutters or unfussy curtains at the windows and investing in a well-upholstered chair and a French or Swedish Gustavian-style bed – or even just a simple divan complete with plumply-upholstered headboard and corresponding satin eiderdown – you can introduce a similar sense of understated luxury into your own home. The one thing you want to avoid in a relaxing space is harsh lighting. Yes, in a bathroom it's likely to be a necessity if, for example,

one shaves or applies makeup here, but confine task lighting to the mirror and choose gentle mood lighting for bathing – a chandelier allows light to diffuse beautifully through its crystals. For storage, free-standing pieces convey an informal feel. The bathroom is another room in which old armoires really come into their own – you can customise their interiors by adding shelves and hooks, if necessary, and many of them are even deep enough to house a chest of drawers.

THE PARED-DOWN VINTAGE BEDROOM

Prefer to see things with a harder edge? This sort of old-world room appeals to more masculine tastes with its unfinished plasterwork, use of metal and utilitarian accessories.

It's the lack of extraneous detail that ensures this sort of room (found in an old house in Florence, Italy) appeals to more low-key tastes. Though the beds feature curlicued wrought iron, its dark colour gives it an edge, cushions are kept to a minimum and the reconditioned 1930s' lamp is simple in form. Above all, it's the unfinished plaster that gives this room its rough-and-ready feel, while in the same home (overleaf) that textured, multi-hued look is taken to an extreme on the walls, giving them a rich, almost golden, look. Indeed, the owner here considers it such a feature that he's even chosen to frame a section of the wall's plaster. Yet, for all its lack of conventional polish, the essentials for a good night's sleep are here: a comfortable bed, a snuggly throw, a lamp – there's even a stove for warmth once the autumnal chill sets in. This is a difficult look to recreate in your own home unless you've got a period property and grand proportions to begin with. Anyone who's taken on a restoration project, though, should find it cheering to see here that it's possible to create atmospheric, beautiful spaces by celebrating less-than-perfect vintage interiors rather than by seeking to bring them up to 21st-century standards.

IF YOU'VE GOT IT, FLAUNT IT

If you've built up a vintage shoe and handbag collection that's worth showing off, there's nothing to stop you using your bedroom walls to store and display your possessions at one and the same time. After all, if they're good enough for your wardrobe, they're good enough for your room.

All sorts of fashion-related items lend themselves to bedroom or bathroom displays. A variety of differently-shaped vintage mirrors can look great in a bathroom while, as shown overleaf, bags and purses – or necklaces, earrings and bracelets for that matter – look fantastic when wall-mounted and grouped by shape or colour. It's a practical option too: it's so much easier to spot the particular item you're looking for when they are all in front of you rather than tucked away in drawers. Choose hooks that are pretty in their own right: many vintage-style options are readily available from mail-order companies, design stores and traditional hardware shops – from the sinuous curves of old French laundry hooks to Mexican tinware and pretty glass-tipped knobs. If your collection comes in the form of textiles or patchwork, keep the decoration elsewhere in the room muted and based around just a few complementary colours so that nothing detracts from the intrinsic beauty of the fabrics themselves. In the photo on the near right, for instance, the owner of the patchwork quilt and cushions has stuck to a montage of black-and-white photos and chosen a bedside table with a warm wooden finish that echoes the colours within the quilt and cushions.

SMALL IS BEAUTIFUL

In a space that's got room for little more than a bed, go to town with a cosy look that features lavish curtains and pretty bedlinens – all in comforting shades of red, plum and pink.

Whatever size your vintage bedroom, it can become a place that engages all your senses. Textiles and a sheepskin rug underfoot can appeal to your sense of touch, a bedside jar containing home-made biscuits can satisfy your sense of taste, while garden roses or scented linen-water give off delicious, sleep-inducing fragrances. And of course the overall design of the room will be visually pleasing too. If, as is the case here, space really is at a premium, a window makes an ideal 'frame' for a bed, drawing the eye beyond the room to give the illusion of more space, with curtains creating a 'four-poster' effect. When choosing or making curtains, the rule with fabric can be quantity, not quality: lavish amounts of inexpensive material will always look better than skimpy pieces of extravagance. If you're someone with expensive tastes, you can indulge your passion with opulent cushions and throws. Remember, in the smaller space, that a little goes a long way – of course you'll want to personalise walls with your favourite artworks but keep these to a minimum if you want to feel truly relaxed: too much art and the effect may look overly 'busy'. And think creatively when it comes to storage: many divan beds – whose less-than-lovely bases can be hidden with valances – feature integral drawers; alternatively items can be stored under the bed. Bookshelves can be arranged around doorways and your prettiest clothes can be hung up on doors, as here, rather than hidden away.

Pattern, texture and colour
ARE THE KEY VINTAGE ELEMENTS

When creating a vintage room, it's all about imaginative and expressive combinations. Vintage paintings, rugs, jewellery, clothes – use them, love them, enjoy them.

CREDITS:

COVER IMAGE FRONT
Photographer Karina Tengberg - Producer Tami Christiansen

COVER IMAGE BACK
Photographer Mikkel Vang - Producer Christine Rudolph

LIVING SPACES
P 7, 8, 10, 11, 18, 20, 21
Photographer Karina Tengberg - Producer Tami Christiansen
P 13, 14, 15
Photographer Mikkel Vang
P 16-17
Photographer Nathalie Krag - Producer Letizia Donati
P 23, 24, 25, 27, 42, 44, 45, 46, 47
Photographer Ngoc Ming Ngo
P 28, 30, 31
Photographer Mikkel Vang - Producer Christine Rudolph
P 33, 34
Photographer Nathalie Krag - Producer Helene Schjerbeck
P 37, 39, 40, 41
Photographer Nathalie Krag - Producer Tami Christiansen
P 49, 50, 51
Photographer Prue Ruscoe - Producer Megan Morton
P 52, 53
Photographer Dana van Leeuwen - Producer Jessica Bouvy

KITCHENS
P 55, 56, 59, 64, 66, 67
Photographer Ngoc Ming Ngo
P 61, 62, 63
Photographer Karina Tengberg - Producer Tami Christiansen
P 69
Photographer Nathalie Krag - Producer Tami Christiansen
P 70
Photographer Mikkel Vang - Producer Christine Rudolph
P 72, 73
Photographer Mikkel Vang

BED & BATHROOMS
P 75, 76, 78, 79
Photographer Mikkel Vang
P 81
Photographer Mikkel Vang - Producer Christine Rudolph
P 83, 84, 85
Photographer Nathalie Krag - Producer Letizia Donati
P 87
Photographer Nathalie Krag - Producer Tami Christiansen
P 88, 89
Photographer Alexander van Berge - Producer Ulrika Lundgrun
P 90, 92, 93, 94, 95
Photographer Bernd Opitz - Producer Gabriella Opitz

All photographers are represented by Taverne Agency.
More of their work can be found on www.taverneagency.com

CONTACTS:

LIVING SPACES
P 7, 8, 9, 10, 11
www.seraoflondon.com
P 12, 13, 14, 15
www.alannahhill.com.au
P 22, 23, 24, 25, 26, 27
www.jonathanadler.com
P 37
www.adrianabarra.com.br
www.micasa.com.br
P 48, 49, 50, 51
www.leemathews.com/au
P 52, 53
www.sachavink.nl

KITCHENS
P 64, 65, 66, 67
www.betseyjohnson.com
P 68, 69
www.shirleyfintz.com
www.monkeybiz.co.za
P 72, 73
www.alannahhill.com.au

BED & BATHROOMS
P 75, 76, 77, 78, 79
www.alannahhill.com.au
P 86, 87
www.adrianabarra.com.br
www.micasa.com.br